The Mirror Makes No Sense

by
Mark Angelo Cummings

Bloomington, IN  Milton Keynes, UK
authorHOUSE

AuthorHouse™
1663 Liberty Drive, Suite 200
Bloomington, IN 47403
www.authorhouse.com
Phone: 1-800-839-8640

AuthorHouse™ UK Ltd.
500 Avebury Boulevard
Central Milton Keynes, MK9 2BE
www.authorhouse.co.uk
Phone: 08001974150

First published by AuthorHouse 3/23/2006

ISBN: 1-4259-2404-2 (sc)

Printed in the United States of America
Bloomington, Indiana

This book is printed on acid-free paper.

Dedication

I am dedicating this book to my lovely wife, who has been a constant in my life. She has been the angel that opened the doors to my heaven, the guiding light of my soul. Like a flower her name fills my heart with joy and laughter. Violet you complete me.

Mark A Cummings

The Mirror Makes No Sense

The intention of the author is to reach out to society, while educating them on a topic that is controversial and with little information known. He hopes to create an interest, while opening doors for families, and their love ones, and provide greater communication on the subject. His experience has been painful, enlightening, and extremely spiritual. No one will ever know what you feel, until they have walked a mile in your shoes. No one will care to understand until it happens to them. Yet, one should always remember that God loves us unconditionally. Human beings are the ones that set conditions, and they are the ones that put the pen on the paper to teach us God's word. I guess they figure, it is easier to reject than to understand. Understanding takes work and a deeper thought process. Over all, one must learn to listen from the heart, disengage the brain and try not to make judgment.

I welcome you to my world, come and stay awhile. If you may read from your heart and learn what you can. I truly hope it makes you a better person in the end. I know that my journey, and the writing of this book, has enlightened me, and has given me a purpose. Please enter my world, share with me my life, my struggles, my inner demons and my beloved angels. Experience my reflection, then and only then, you will see why, the mirror made no sense......

In The Beginning

One last push Mrs. Perdomo, you are almost there. Mother's sweat pored down her forehead, as she attempts her last push. "Good job", said Doctor Robles, a man in his fifties, the wrinkles on his forehead expressed his travels and hard life. "It's a beautiful baby girl". He gently placed me on my mother's arms. Mr. and Mrs. Perdomo were delighted, all her fingers and toes were there. "She is perfect and healthy". Mr. Perdomo exclaimed while he smiled and touched little Maritza's hand. I looked around in distress, my big round brown eyes popping out of my head, "wait a minute, did some one say girl. What girl, someone must have made a terrible mistake here, he must have made a wrong call. He meant boy, a handsome and strong boy. Back up, rewind, hey doctor, call it again, I am boy, not a girl." All these years inside my head and in my heart, I've seen myself as a boy, a man. Yet they said I was born a "girl"?

Ok, so it didn't quite happen like that, obviously I couldn't talk then, for crying out loud, I didn't know what a boy or a girl was, infants in general know no gender. It's a shame that genitals are the leading factor for the marker on your drivers license. Yes, I was given a female name, dressed, and raised as a girl, but to tell you the truth, I never really felt like one. I hated the dresses, the dolls, all that girly stuff. It was a nightmare, a never ending one. Until 38 years later, I discovered what was wrong with me, I had gender disphoria. So you are asking yourself what is that? Well, here goes: gender disphoria in short is when you mind and body do not match. You see yourself as the opposite sex from the reflection in the mirror.

Hence, the mirror makes no sense. No, were not crazy, demented or confused. We don't need the exorcist, nor a shrink. This is a real disorder, a birth defect. Trust me, it sucks. How would you like to get up in the morning, look down at your privates and oops, they were gone. There you are, all your life thinking you were a male, every breath, every beat of your heart is thumping "I am a man". Yet, you woke up one morning you guessed it, with a vagina, getting clearer? As hard as it is to understand, we're not freaks. We are regular human beings with a chromosome problem. Mother nature played an awful trick on us, or she must have had too much to drink the night before. Either way, it's no picnic. This condition is world wide, there are over 2 million transsexual males and females in the world and the numbers are climbing. Why haven't you heard about this before? Because society looks down on people like us, almost like the plague. They think we are freaks, defiantly behaved individuals, that have nothing else better to do than to change their sex. They keep us underground, not providing much needed information and treatment to help us integrate in to society. Religion plays a major role in our isolation, by preaching hateful remarks and alienating us from our community. Instead of embracing Gods creation, and understanding the logistics of our disease.

As a child I could never understand why I could not urinate standing up like my father. "Ok, lets try this again, bring the pants down grab my privates and aim. Oh-oh, I did it again, piss kept dripping down my leg. Why can't I get it inside the toilet? I must ask dad, how he does it." To my disappointment, after many years, I figured out I won't ever get it right, I had the wrong equipment. A child's mind is so complex, we have ways of make believing till it becomes true in our minds. Yet grown ups can be so cruel, and with little compassion and understanding. "Maritza, you are not a boy, you are a girl, stop acting like one". Mother yelled for the hundredth time. Haydee was a beautiful woman, proud and coy. Her skin was ivory soft, her eyes were green and vibrant with a sad look that overshadowed her soul. All her life she dreamed about having a girl, she wanted a best friend, a confidant. So, obviously I was a disappointment to her from the very start. She went out of her way to make me look and act like a girl. Mother had special dresses made for me, they were extremely girly with all the ruffles and bows. I wanted to wear pants and shorts, and of coarse, no top. I wanted to bare my chest, like my dad. The dolls she gave me, quickly became cars. As I moved them across the table. I would envy my neighbors, the boys across the way, who got to play, and rough it, as I could only dream about. When playing house, I always wanted to play the man, every role had to be masculine. No ballerina or nurse for me, I had to be a fireman or a doctor. The disphoria hunted my every being. I could never quite understand why my body was different from the boys, but my mother quickly reminded me, that I was born a girl. I was born in Havana Cuba, the communist regime was going strong. We struggled like everyone else did, barely having enough to eat. However, my father may have had many shortcomings, but one of his greatest virtues, was the ability to provide food on the table. They both wanted the best for their baby "girl". "Maritza, don't get dirty, that's a brand new dress you have on, you know girls don't play that way." Mother was such a nag, God forbid I would have any fun. Although Castro stripped every thing we owned, my parents still managed to keep some dignity and pride in our home. Mother was very clean, in excess it seemed. Things had to be kept neat and tidy, no questions asked. This was her way of controlling our world. Although my memories are vague, I do remember my home, my neighborhood, and some distinctive faces. The morning we were getting ready to leave Cuba is very vivid in my mind. Everyone was running around frantic, I was not sure why all the commotion. Suddenly, a knock on the door, a man in green fatigues, came and took us away. We were placed on an airplane, since then, I never returned to the place I called home. I was scared, confused, why did we leave? I had to learn a new language, a new way of life.

People were different here, they seemed cruel and uncaring. My parents weren't happy, they had to work all the time. The arguments got worse through the years. My father drank heavily, and appeared to have a heavy hand. I cringed every time he walked through the door, his speech was slurred, his temper high. All mother had to do was ask a question, and things would start flying through the air. I cried and shivered, hiding, wanting him to stop. He would hit her, time and time again. Only to apologize once the demon left his veins.

At first, my father did not come with us on the plane, Castro had him working on the sugar cane fields, so it wasn't until 6 months later that he was allowed to leave Cuba. I remember crying for him every night, could not wait to read his letters, hovering over the mail man when the mail would come in. If only I new the turn of events, I would have wished, he would have never come to the US. I was placed in school, having to learn and deal with a culture I was not ready for. The kids were cruel, they would call me names. Spick, was a usual word for those that were not native of the US. Go back to Cuba they would say. I was made fun of all the time, four eyes, cross eyed, I was called every name in the book. The one thing that hurt the most is when they would call me a girl. I wanted to play with the boys, be part of their club. But they were quick to say, we don't play with girls. This curse, was to be with me for a very long time.

The years went buy and I was forced to adapt to their world. I had to play their game, being mommies little girl. It was a struggle growing up. I could not relate to anyone around me, I was withdrawn, always wanting to be alone. I would listen to music, and recreate a world in my mind. It was an escape, I could be whom I wanted. Boys really never appealed to me, except that I envied there bodies, I wanted to have what they had, the body to match my brain. Instead I had to live the life of a lesbian, my moms worst nightmare. Although, I did make several attempts to be "normal", I could never fit the bill. I dated a few guys, experimenting my mothers theory, "once you go out with boys you will like them". I even managed to get married. She was wrong, I didn't like them. Although I was curious, I did want to learn more about them, after all I had no good male role models. Poor dad, you have got to love him, he was a good disciplinarian, and provider, he yelled and threw things around, but was definitely not much of a good role model. The bottle always had the best of him. Eventually they divorced, I actually saw it coming, it was really only a matter of time. Did I mention I was not an only child, I have a sister and a brother, we were all born 8 years apart. I guess after me they were weary about having more children, not knowing what to expect. Why is it that parents always think that they are the victims, do they for once, see beyond themselves? If they could only realize that their role in life is not to screw us up, but to facilitate our path and to help us grow. Not to control, disrupt or change our journeys. They can really mess things up. I have always thought there should be a manual, "Parenting For Dummies".

I wonder if they do things on purpose, wanting to have children, so that they can control them, screw them up, and teach them to do the same to their children. So, by now you must think I hate my parents, well your wrong. I actually love them very much. My mother is the apple of my eye. I have always wanted to make her happy, although it was an impossible task. Nothing could ever please her, no matter how hard I tried. I think this is one of my biggest problems in life, well at least one of them. My obsessive compulsive nature, stems from lack of approval. If she would have only read the manual. "Maritza come straighten out your drawers", my mother yelled as she frantically threw the clothes on the floor. If things weren't align the way her neurotic mind saw them, then I had to do it all over again, until it was right. I grew up with this torture, it was very scary. I still torture myself this way, I have what they call obsessive compulsive disorder. Everything has to be in a set order, or its not right. Many nights I lay awake, thinking of the terrible things I had to go through as a child. To be loved and accepted for who I was, became an obsession. So much so, that I confused friendship with sex, and in order to feel accepted, there were many times that I gave myself up, to feel loved. I was molested several times, mostly by my parent's, so called friends, feeling betrayed and unprotected, a worthless piece of trash. I had really low self esteem, lacked self love, and had no dignity. I started to experiment with drugs and alcohol. It was a way out, an escape from reality. My body was my enemy, it did not belong to me, so maybe if I abused it long enough, I would get a new one, or so I had hoped. As I got older, my female frame, became more apparent, I hated every part of it. The breasts, annoyed and frustrated me. They were a stranger to my frame. If I could only get rid of them, I would be happy. But every morning there they were, bigger and firmer than ever. No one new of my distress, my anger, and my frustration. Why was I given this torture, this plague.

My mother continued to haunt my every existence. If I dressed the way I wanted, which of coarse was masculine, she would torment and made fun off me. Everything had to be her way. I was to be her doll, her mannequin to parade at her demand. My gentle nature did not allow me to put her in her place. After all she was my mother, the one who gave birth to me. At times I wanted so bad to send her to hell, but deep inside I new I could not do that. I could never hurt her, not like that. So I continued to please her, as much as I could. There was an angel in my life, my wonderful grandmother, however, she too wanted me to be a girl. But she was different, more loving. She had kinder words to say. How could a person so loving give birth to some one so demanding and conditional. It was almost like they were not related. But they were. To love is an art, one that must me mastered. Not everyone is meant to be an artist. Grandma was influenced by her religion, after grandpa died, she devoted her life to God, it was her calling. Sunday morning early to rise, knocking on peoples door to preach the awakening, Armageddon was getting near. She tried oh so desperately to convert me, she wanted my salvation, and in her mind this would be the only way. It is sad that people take their agendas and their morals and make them into religion. Don't they realize God loves us unconditionally, they always forget that real important part during their preaching. I truly think religion was started to help control man kind. After all, prior to any form of strict religion we were unruly. So in a sense its good to have rules and regulations, even if its plagued with guilt. Church has become a business, a place were people go repent, only to go back and do it all over again. But as long as you pay, and confess, then I guess you are ok. As an adult, I have very little tolerance for religion. I see all the evil that is connected with it. The wars, the killing, the separation between countries. It originated as something good, man has made it evil. It is used to hurt, offend, and outcast love ones. Families are torn apart because of religion. Why do we keep following outdated material, there are new exceptions, new stories to tell. Well enough of that subject. Let see, you know about grandma, by the way she passed in 1996, it was my first loss ever. Needless to say, I became very depressed and had to go on anti depressants. I miss her, yet wonder what her response to my transition might have been. Who knows, she loved me so much that I think she would have understood. More than I can say for my mother, its been almost 2 years since my transition, and she still calls me by my female name. I truly think she will never come around. I hope I am wrong. In some sick and tremendously sad way, I feel I need her approval, her recognition. I want her to say that I am her son. Yet, she is dense, hard headed and can't see beyond herself. She insists that I am her daughter, with my hairy chest and all. If for once, she could understand me, feel my pain. Truly find her heart and love for me, I think she could finally accept me as her son. After all she did give birth to me, Mark the man, the boy who yearns for his mother's love. Funny, I thought my father would have had a harder time dealing with my transition. He is actually good with it. A man with less than a 5th grade education, in Cuba, has better sense, than a women with a bookkeeping degree. Goes to show you, education isn't everything.

Well growing up was not easy. I was confused, angry, felt unloved and misunderstood. I really never felt pretty, because I wanted to be handsome. I felt awkward, and out of place. I had problems making friends, and never felt I belonged. But with Gods grace, I manage to grow up and function. No suicide, although I can't say I didn't try. Overall I turned out to be a productive adult. I did however, have a few bumps on the road. I became addicted to drugs, was displaced in many homes, and lost many jobs. I had problems finding myself, and you can see why.

Now that you know a little bit of my background, lets go forward, oh, lets say to my teenage years. This was the first time I contemplated a sex change. I was 17, and fell in love with my high school sweet heart.

Denise Whitus was a classmate of my mine, we were in theatre class, and became very close friends. I fell deeply in love with her. It wasn't her looks, but her personality. She was sweet, gentle, fun loving and very outgoing. We had a lot in common. We both shared the love for the theatre, acting, and the drama. Every day that passed by, I fell deeper in love with her. We were together all the time. After a while, she stopped seeing her boyfriend, because all her time was spent with me. There was one problem, she didn't like girls. She was straight, I could see that off the bat. But some how I won her over, and the friendship got deeper. She fell in love with me, but could not deal with the fact that I had a female body. Hey, for that matter, neither could I. My aura was that of a man, my every essence was manly. I wanted so bad to have a sex change, we even created a name for me, Michael. I figured having a sex change would end all of our problems, I could marry Denise, and we would live happily ever after. Yeah, I was dreaming again. First, I could never afford the surgery, this was something they did in another country. Second, they weren't even that successful then, we are talking back in 1980. So instead I had to deal with my anguish. Eventually Denise's parents found out about our affair, and she was sent away to California, never to be found again.

I was heart broken and lost for many years. I eventually recovered, but never forgot my first love, and the gut wrenching pain I felt at the time. I put off the thought of getting a sex change until 2003. In the mean time I had to live my life as a Lesbian. I had no other choice. I was in and out of so many relationships, never finding happiness.

Finding Myself

Everything and everyone left a void in my heart. All the relationships I had weren't fulfilling, I felt I was living a lie. I longed to feel normal. I knew I didn't like men. So, that was definitely out of the question. Oh don't get me wrong, I did try. Been there, done that. As hesitant as I am about revealing this part of my life, it is part of it. First there was Tom, a nice guy I met at work. He knew I liked girls, but decided to give us a try. We were both looking for a place to live, so we became roommates, with benefits. I felt really bad, I gave him false hope. I tried, but I just couldn't stomach it. It seemed that every chance I had, I would try to be that good girl, my mother wanted me to be. So I kept trying, "maybe mom is right I just need to find the right guy." But every time, I kept hitting my head against the same wall. I like females, I don't like men. I like smooth skin, breast, long hair and nails. So definitely, Tom did not meet the criteria.

Then there was Fred. An English "gentleman" who promised to sweep me of my feet, with his British accent, and lies about his past and present. Once again, I tried, but failed. This is a book on it own, "my journey in the UK". It was like being in the twilight zone. I was married to Fred for 3 months, our marriage was annulled. I found myself all alone in a foreign country. I battled the weather, hunger, fear, and lack of security. But I had too much pride to ask for help from home. I refused to hear my nagging mother's remarks. The marriage didn't work out, obviously, due to lack of sexual participation. I couldn't even consummate it. So off to court I went, in front of white wigged hair men, who accused me of being a lesbian, and leading on, poor old Fred. Well poor he was, a poor bastard, bus driver, who didn't even have a dime to his name. He was 55, and at the time I was 24. He had lied to me about his age, he told me he was 40. He also said he had never been married, and that he worked for the government. Well, it turned out I was his 3rd wife, and he had three children. He worked for the government alright, he was a bus driver. He didn't even own the house he lived in. Well after learning all the lies, I was disgusted and ready to head out the door. I of coarse was unable to sleep with him, because of all the lies, and a small technicality, "he was a man". I had been honest with him, I told him the truth, that I had been with girls all my life. But I was willing to give us a try, he just had to be patient with me. He had agreed. But once I found out all the lies, you can bet your bottom dollar, he screwed all the chances he had to sleep with me. I left his place, and fended for myself. If there is one thing I cant stand are liars. I don't cheat nor lie, and I have no patients for those that do. To make a long story short, I stayed in England for 2 years, till all the hype died down back home. So you ask why did you marry a 55 year old man? At the time I was in a bad relationship, and highly involved in drugs. My mother had gotten into a very bad car accident. She begged me to marry Fred and turn my life around. Like a good daughter once again, I listened and gave in to her demands. You can't imagine my mothers' fury when I called her and told her I could no longer be with Fred.

Needless to say, I continued leading empty relationships. I was like an addict trying desperately to find love, or even the perfect relationship. But, I always fell short and was disappointed. Little did I know it was not the relationship, it was the image in the mirror that made no sense. I was the one that needed to change. My outside needed to match my insides. I was lost, I felt broken, it wasn't till I was 38 years old, when my life finally took a right turn. I met the most amazing female. She was different, not like the other girls I had known. She was special, something about her allowed me to be myself. She was straight and had lived with men all her life. Yet, she was curious about girls, having had a few encounters in the past, but nothing too serious. We met at Ballys. I could feel her presence, she would stare at me for hours at a time, during my work outs at the gym. One day she actually approached me in the girls locker room. Introducing herself to me, "Hi my name is Violet, and I like girls". I thought it was an awkward introduction, but effective. From that day on it was history. We went on a few dates, then after a few months, we moved in together. It was however, a challenging relationship. I am old fashion and controlling, your typical Latino male. She was like a wild horse, untamed, did not like being told what to do. We struggled at first, yet it was promising, after finally working out the quirks, we managed to have smooth sailing, well for the most part. She had been in a long term relationship with another guy. But things weren't so great between them. As a matter of fact, they were rooming it for the past few years. They had some crazy arrangement, until I came along. After a rough couple of months, she moved out of their place, and moved in with me.

We fell in love, and decided nine months into the relationship to get married. It was a beautiful ceremony in Key West, Florida. As you know "gay" couples are not allowed to get legally married, but that didn't stop me, I wanted to show her I loved her. So like every proud gay couple we forked out the bucks to perform a pseudo marriage. A certificate, a bottle of champagne, photos, and a two hour cruise at sunset. A notary performed the ceremony. We spend an enjoyable week in the keys. It was a great experience. The most prevalent of all things, was my new found knowledge of the transsexual world. Where we stayed, there were a couple of girls who mention the fact, that I looked like an FTM. This means female to male in the transgender world. When a female transforms or transcends into a male, via hormone, surgeries or both. I was curious and exited at the same time. Was there such a world? Was there hope for me yet? When we got home from our honeymoon, the research began, and boy did I learn. My skies opened up, for the first time in my life I felt hope. I can't express in words the feeling that came over me, to see others like me right in front of my very eyes, thanks to the information highway, the internet. Why was this information not available to me at seventeen? Tears came rolling down my eyes, I wanted to scream, I wanted to shout. I was angry, happy and anxious all at the same time. I wanted this, and I wanted it now. I felt like I had been in a capsule for years, stuck in time, and all of a sudden I got out.

Time is ticking, that is all I kept thinking. I have got to do this now. Site after site, I couldn't get enough information. Transgender mania, the world wide web, all at my fingertips. How come I didn't know about this before. Have I been living under a rock. Talk about being at the right place, at the right time. If it weren't for my wedding, I would have probably never found out about this transmen's world. I was so exited, like a kid with a new toy. Thoughts kept racing in my head. How will I be able to spring this on my family, clients, and friends. What, do I just come out and say it. "I am going to become a man". Right, lets bring out the white jacket and strap you up. This was going to take some thinking, planning, and careful consideration. First things first, what is the first step?

As I gathered more information, I noted it wasn't going to be as easy as I thought it would be. I had to schedule an appointment with a psychiatrist. They would have to determine if I suffered from gender dysphoria. I would have to prove that this was not a fad. Sounds like my mother was directing these sessions. One hundred and fifty bucks a session, that sounds kind of steep, to sit or lay on a couch and tell someone: "God played a terrible joke on me, I am actually a man". I definitely looked like one. I had the hard features and the fuzz on my upper lip. I had been shaving for a while now, to avoid controversy with my clients and friends, but as soon as I found out that I was going to transition, I started to let my mustache grow. I had taken prohormones to build up my physique for bodybuilding, which created some facial hairs and manly features. I had been diligently working out and creating a more masculine physique. So I knew I would not have a problem passing or getting Docs approval. So off to the psychiatrist I went.

My hands began to sweat, I was nervous and scared. What if she denies my transition? What if my mother manages to screw this up for me? All these terrible thoughts kept popping in my head. I nervously flipped the pages of the magazines, inside the waiting room. The door finally opened, "Maritza Cummings"? A tall, slender women, with a gentle smile on her face, approached me and welcomed me into her office. I could feel my teeth clenching, the sweat on my forehead, my heart was excessively pounding. She then proceeded to ask me questions. How long have you known of your dysphoria? Are you in a relationship right now? I felt like a guest on one of those daytime talk shows, being drilled with questions. My head was pounding, I kept trying to tell myself to relax. I would answer her questions, and felt myself gasping for air. "I hope she doesn't think something is wrong with me". Before I knew it, the hour was up. She seemed pleased with the interrogation. "We will set up the next appointment, and continue with our sessions." She said as she pulled out her scheduling book. I am thinking here, ok lady, how long are we doing this for. I am not a fan of the psychiatry world. Just give me the paper and I will be on my way. I hinted in a round about way, "So, how many sessions does it take to prove I have gender dysphoria?" She reassured me that it wouldn't take that many sessions, she had no doubt of my dysphoria. All she wanted to know was if I was well adjusted, and could go through surgery. That was definitely reassuring. At one hundred and fifty dollars a session, I was really hoping this would not be a long ordeal. After 5 sessions, which seemed like a life time to me, I finally got my letter. We had a few sessions with Violet, she wanted to make sure I was in a happy relationship. I passed with flying colors, there was never a doubt.

Next, was setting up an appointment with a surgeon. This was going to take special planning and research. Unfortunately, there are not many surgeons involved in changing ones sex. It's almost like finding a needle in a hay stack. But I have always been a determined individual, so hunting I went. There were several options, but not all local. Of coarse, I went with the local ones. Having my own business made it difficult to just pick up and go. If I don't work, I don't get paid, and that could be a problem. The price for these surgeries, almost gave me a heart attack. The grand total for changing a vagina into a penis, removing the breast, creating body and facial hair, deepening the voice, would be a grand total of at least $200,000. I would have to say, a bit much. It would have to be done in stages, and hope I win the lotto. After several consultations, I decided to go with our local Cleveland Clinic. A state of the art facility, with good doctors, and a decent reputation. The project would be to remove the breast and all of the female pluming. Go on hormones, and pray that it all goes well. I set up the appointment and patiently waited.

My palms were sweaty, my heart raced. I was finally going in for my surgical consultation. Would this be the man that will make my dreams come true. Would this be the person that allows me to be born again. For a moment, the world stood still, I could see the small child being held in my mothers arms. It's a boy, it's a beautiful baby boy. My mother smiled and kissed my forehead. "Mrs. Cummings," I was awakened by a short blonde haired lady, I entered Dr. Boyd's office. By now you are probably wondering, from Perdomo, how did we get to Cummings. Well lets see, my fathers last name was Perdomo, then I changed it to Golding, Freds' last name. Then to Cummings, my last girl friends last name, prior to Violet. I changed my last name legally to hers. I didn't want to keep Fred's last name any longer, and I was never happy with Perdomo.

Dr Boyd appeared to be an excellent surgeon with good bedside manners. After showing him a few pictures of what I wanted my chest to look like, he assured me, he could do the job. I was his first female to male chest reconstruction surgery. Normally, I would have been worried, but he appeared to be an artist, a man that could take on a challenge. We then discussed the need to get all my female organs out at once, which led me to set up an appointment with the gynecological surgeon, Dr Davila. I had been having pains in my pelvic region for quite a while now, I suspected I had fibroids and cysts inside my ovaries. Ever since I was a teenager, I always had the worst cramping and abnormal menstrual cycles. So, I knew it wouldn't be an issue to have a full hysterectomy. We set up a date, my new birthday, December 22,

2003. I couldn't believe it, what I waited for my entire life, was going to finally take place.

Before my surgeries, there were a lot of lose ends to tie up. I had to manage a few things in my business and personal life. After all, I could die on the operating table. As you well know, any kind of surgery is dangerous, but sex reassignment surgery is complicated. Imagine, bilateral mastectomy (removal of the breast tissue) nipple grafting, along with the removal of all my female reproductive organs, to include the uterus, fallopian tubes, ovaries and cervix. This was no 2 hour surgery, this would take along time, more like 7 hours. I knew the risks I was putting myself through, but it was a small price to pay, to fix my life long birth defect. I Mark Angelo Cummings, will finally be. No more pretending or dreaming, the moment will soon be here. The man in the making, the man that was overdue, is finally arriving. The mirror will soon become clearer.

The day had finally arrived. I was nervous, yet excited. Violet held my hand, as they placed the intravenous injection in my arm. She kissed me and couldn't keep her eyes off of me. I sensed her fears, she was happy for me, but I knew she was afraid that she will never see me again. A bitter sweet moment, Maritza will soon be gone, but Mark, her man will soon come home. She was trying to stay cool, not act nervous. She was trying to be strong for both of us. Yet, I new she was afraid and felt the grief in her heart. I, on the other hand, was at peace. I felt if I die, I will die a man. I could go home to my heavenly father with pride and honor. Life would not be worth living as a women, I was tired of the lies. Finally, I was making it right, and soon, I could make Violet my real wife. We could proudly present ourselves in society, walk with our heads high, as Mr. and Mrs. Cummings.

Dr. Boyd came in, ask me if I was ready, and proceeded to draw lines on my chest. The construction will soon begin. There is a man in the making, there is work to be done. Violet and I gently kissed, our eyes locked, our souls held tight, as they rolled me in to the operating room. It was cold and bright, the beginning of the end, a place were a new life begins and another ends. I felt a burning sensation in my arm as the anesthesia entered my blood stream. I felt myself fall into a trance, goodbye Maritza my old friend, I slowly went into a deep sleep. Yet, I could see her from a distance, walking away. For a moment my life and memories all flashed before my very eyes. Every memory I ever had quickly stood before me. Maritza smiled and waived goodbye, she had tears rolling from her eyes, with a bitter sweet look of relief. She new she did not belong there, in that body she had called home for years. She walked away and vanished, never to be seen again. Mark waived goodbye, and whispered, "thank you for letting me come home".

The doctors worked diligently, cutting and carving away, changing a life, creating a man, aligning a body and soul. Making something very right. Let there soul forever be in peace, for if they have ever done work this meaningful, it has never been recognized and appreciated, until now. Job well done men. My eyes opened, I soon found out that I was alive. Everything must have gone right. There was a nurse next to me, I asked her, what time it was, she said, 7 pm. I went into surgery at 10:30 in the morning, how can it be 7 pm? My mind started to race, did something go wrong? She wasn't much help though, actually she was rather rude. Little did I know it was the beginning of prejudice in my transsexual world. To this day it puzzles me, that people who are suppose to be educated, and in the medical field, can find ways of being prejudice, with someones birth defect. I asked her were my wife was, she muttered, she cant come inside the recovery room, you will see her shortly when they take you to your room. It seemed like an eternity, but finally, at last, I saw Violet. She was relieved, I was drugged out of my mind, between the anesthesia and the morphine they gave me, I was stooped. I felt like a mummy, all bandaged up and wrapped. I proceeded to touch my chest, "they were gone, they were actually gone". I smiled, I finally got rid of them. I ached and itched all over, yet nothing mattered, I was finally the man that I was born to be. Little did I know that the surgery was actually the easy part, recovering, well that's another story. To make a long story short. They kept me in the hospital for 3 days, it was Christmas eve. One holiday season I will never forget. Which reminds me, never, ever, schedule a surgery over the Christmas holidays. They have limited staffing, which means you get a bunch of new comers, nurses that don't know what they are doing. To give you an example, my catheter had to be put back in, since I couldn't urinate on my own. It took two nurses and finally a physician to get it right. Pain is not the word, try excruciating torture. Also, finding a vein to draw blood, you would have had, better luck finding a needle in a hay stack, then the nurses drawing blood, without committing murder. I was not a happy camper. If it weren't for the euphoria I felt, I would have had someone's head in a platter. I managed to urinate on my own, Alleluia, there is a God.

Walking, sitting, and laying down are things we take for granted. After surgery, these things took a lot of effort. Thank God for Violet, she once again proved to be my guardian angel. Always by my side taking care of her man. The recovery was long and painful. I still don't understand how anyone in their right mind thinks being transgender is a fad or deviant behavior. As if we have nothing else better to do than to risk our lives, go through painful procedures and change our lives a full 360. Heck why not, nothing else better to do. The hardest thing after surgery was the lack of physical activity I was allowed to do. I was use to working out daily, running my personal training studio, and having an overall active life. All of which came to a complete halt.

The months went buy, and my strength and activity levels increased. I was able to tend to my business with full force. The challenge lied on explaining my transition to those that once new me, or educating the new ones to come. I have never felt the need to keep my transition a secret. My spiritual side has always guided me to educate others and open up their hearts and minds. If I where to just blend in, then what would be the purpose. What good would it do to go through it all. Selfishly, to camouflage myself and be just another productive citizen of the state. No, that's not me. I Mark Angelo Cummings, have a greater plan, a destiny to fulfill. If every transgender man and women, refused to tell their story, other lost souls would not be found. I want to help my fellow transmen and women, to have a loving and productive life. To not feel ashamed of whom they are. To blossom, enrich their every existence and grow without fear, shame or limits. We are human beings with feelings and have every right to be here. Gender bending, transcending, being who you were born to be. Life without limits, self expression, all to beautiful to keep hidden and trapped within. Our society needs to grow. Our parents need to open up their horizons and allow their children to evolve. To many borders, to many rules, antiquated, purposeless, creating separation, hate and above all destruction. Its time to grow, to leave the past were it belongs. We need a change, a new horizon, no more guilt ridden passageways. The circle is getting old, lets pave a new direction, one filled with love, understanding and no prejudice. No more hate, let color, gender, and race be all one. The years keep ticking by, and we are still the same. Blood shed, emptiness, destruction, are never changing, lets try a new path. Lets allow religion to be what it was intended to be. The church a place of worship, a safe heaven, a place of love, the structure for all good things. Instead of the reason for wars, separation, hate, prejudice, conditions and overall guilt ridden fools, who shamefully use the name of God with their poisoned tongues to harm and control all. Work with kindness, not with fear, plant a garden without thorns and boundaries.

Being A Man

Now, Mark is a man. No question about it. Although some pluming is still missing, another dreaded procedure in the future to come, nevertheless, he is a real man. Yet, no one taught him what a man is all about. No guided steps, as you would guide a young child through his growing years. Growing up the opposite gender, being told to be a girl, definitely, did not help his new path. So, Mark will have to learn each day that goes by, to be a man every one would love and feel proud off. Being a man has many factors and inscriptions. Characteristics and traits that will carefully be molded and created with each passing day. A man takes up space, is loud, and roars like the lion. Makes no excuse for his mannerism, boldness and overall presence. He is a man. However, there needs to be a balance, a very careful balance. A man can be kind, warm, loving, a father figure. There is a time, and a place for every emotion. Too soft, and you are taken for a fool, to harsh and you are categorized as a brut. So a fine line to walk on, like a tight rope on a circus stage, is the only way. Learn young Mark, for the world is yours for the taking. You have a gift that many envy. You have been given a life of multitude. You now possess the true yin and yang of the world. Once a women, now a man, a beautiful collage of memories and experiences to be used to help mankind.

My business revolves around helping individuals reach their ultimate fitness and health goals. A path, that I chose, as part of the need to achieve full circle. I grow, when I help others grow. So call it karma, if you will. We all need to feel complete, in one way or the other. We all go through life searching for our path. Some get closer, others spin their wheels. Everyday is like a step on the long stairwell that leads us to our destiny. We hope that we never fall, but we keep paving our paths while helping others pave theirs. I truly believe, that my transition has a purpose, beyond just my happiness. The bigger picture here is helping man kind see their true nature. A mirrored reflection to their inner lost soul. Learning to accept differences, embracing it, bringing out the best and learning from the worst. To see the Godliness of our being, to nurture our inner child. Tapping into the energy source that feeds our every existence. Uniting the web that we spew during our daily encounters. Making man kind richer spiritually, and less focused on his riches. That is the plan, that is the coarse. How I will achieve this, is in his hands. I am but a mere servant, his devoted vessel, never questioning, only following his command. The mirror is a canvas, to both our inner and outer being. It's reflection can be changed, especially if you are not happy with it's image. The journey is yours to take, make the change, and everything else will follow.

A Childs Mind

We know no gender, the word boy or girl was incased in our dictionary by our ancestors. During that era, they had little to no entertainment, so finding ways to make things fit nicely in a little box, was a past time. If you were to do your home work there are millions of children born with various genital birth defects.

From an unfinished penis, to multiple heads, these are just a few of the phenomenon seen. Boys have been known to be born with missing testicles, or some have the pleasure of owning three. For that matter we have seen girls born without ovaries, and find themselves very under developed during puberty, and unable to bare children. These are things that happen. Call it fate, pesticides, or drugs administered during, or before pregnancy. You name it, no one particular reason. A birth defect is a birth defect, which ever way you slice it. So when our doctors very proudly call it, as they call the time of death, it's a boy or it's a girl, we can generally wipe our behinds, with their new found findings. Genitals do not make you a man or a women. The brain is what dictates who you are. There are multitudes of research that show gender dysphoria is caused by an imbalance in hormones during the formation of the fetus at 8 weeks time. This happens even in the animal kingdom, were we see this gender mix up. Female fishes and birds take on masculine traits due to toxins they were exposed to. This is a real disorder, 10% of the population are affected. Sexual organs should not be the sole nominator for our gender identity.

Children like to explore and as you often see, they play and emulate roles on a daily basis. Little boys like to wear their mommies shoes, gracefully walking with them as they try on her new lipstick. Panic sets in, the homophobe center quickly responds. Father grabs the shoes and wipes the face, here have a football instead. This in hopes that little Larry will be the next best quarter back. How damaging and ignorant is this. A Child's brain center develops through his or her actions. You can really stunt their development, by interfering in their role play. God forbid, Larry's brain is of a woman, and his body just did not respond during the 8 weeks, inside his mother's womb. What if little Larry has gender dysphoria, a birth defect. Larry's father could really scar him for life, instead of accepting his son for who he, or technically, she is. We spend our lives wanting children. Carefully planning their lives. "No," parents hear this. You do not plan their lives, you are meant to guide and facilitate their journey. Your children are not your puppets, or possessions, you were given a gift from God to bring into this world a human being. Not a robot that you can program as you wish. Children are very precious, and we can learn a lot from them. They are not prejudice, until you teach them that trait. They love without condition, until you condition them. How dare you screw up, what God so carefully created. You take away their true nature and pollute their minds, with your way of thinking and your set of values. For once can you think beyond yourself. Free will, sounds familiar, yes allow him or her to have free will. Guide them yes, keep them away from trouble, due teach them right from wrong, but allow them to develop as they see fit.

Its not hard really, to love without strings and demands. To appreciate the true beauty of self. To understand that pink looks good on any gender, and heels are for whom wants to wear them. It's amazing how freeing it really is, to allow others to be themselves. To stop placing your wants and needs first. To accept the unacceptable, it makes a much better world. Innocence comes and goes. The merry go round will never stop spinning, your first toy will always stay in your heart. Let it be the toy you really want, not the one your parents chose for you. Ask before you buy, you might be surprised what you will hear. But do not judge, nor redirect. Just enjoy, sit back and watch a little being develop into a happy and well centered adult.

Growing up was very confusing. Never really knowing why I couldn't express my true nature. Constantly being redirected or told that everything I did was wrong. Sit this way, don't cross your legs, stand like a lady, don't get dirty, on and on and on....

After awhile a child becomes frustrated, spirit broken, and totally confused. You are who you are, can people see that. Psychologically scarred for life, is the result of intrusive parents that want to mold their child's self being, gender development, and mannerism. I wanted cars, they gave me dolls. I wanted to wear pants, they clothes me in dresses. Everything against my will, against the grain of the wood. You can't change who you are, a tree that is born with a crooked trunk will never straighten. The brain dictates your mannerism, your gender, not your genitals, or what the outside may illustrate. That old saying, you can't judge a book by its cover, well, you can't judge a man by his genitals.

Maritza was a beautiful name, so distant and unfamiliar it sounds, as the word spews my lips. Mark, although very new and recent, feels more at home, more in its place. What I would give to have my childhood again. In the right body, or with parents that were more in tune with my development. Mother nature was cruel, but things do happen. Its up to the parents to make a smooth transition, to see the signs, and comfort our journey. If there is gender in question, allow the child to be who they feel they are. Don't sway or alter in any way, don't mess with perfection. I close my eyes and envision little Mark running in the park. He is playing with his car in hand. Smiling at his parents, with confidence, he jumps and tumbles to the ground. The sun shinning on his face, no one can harm him now. No one telling him that his movements are wrong, that the way he stands, talks or moves are of another gender. Mark is the boy he was born to be. That my friends is how it should have been. Instead Maritza was always afraid, she did not jump, run, or execute any confidence. Maritza was always fearful. To this day, Mark has had to learn to eliminate fear from his life. A fear that was instilled in childhood. Always second guessing his calls, because he was always being redirected in life. Parents please be careful, don't let religion, society, and so call taboos, dictate how you raise your child. Listen to your heart, and let your child's development blossom. A word of advise, please be very careful who you bring into your home. A child is precious and their innocence can be robbed in an instant. Looking back at my childhood. My parents had a dear friend, or should I say a dear friend of my beloved grandfather whom I was too young to remember, before he passed. This man who has since passed himself, molested me at a tender age of eight. I remember it well, as if it were yesterday. I was home sick from school, it was almost as if he had it planned. He knocked on our door and I let him in. He was no stranger, he frequently visited our home. He started to talk to me about sex, and that he and my parents were very special friends, and being special friends they showed their love to each other by having sex. I was eight, but I knew what sex was, after all we are children not dummies. He proceeded to touch me, and said that I was his special friend to, and that he wanted to share with me, what he shared with my parents. At first I was apprehensive, but having no self esteem, and hating my body, I figured, what the heck. What can he do to me, that life hasn't already done. That man stole my innocence. He never really tried to penetrate me, but he would fondle me, have me touch him and performed oral sex. He would give me money and gifts. This went on for years. Until I was disgusted with the whole concept, and did not allow him to continue. I never told my parent until many years later. I figured they wouldn't believe me or would blame me for the incident. So basically what I am getting at, trust no one, not even your closest friends. They will still your child's' heart and innocence. I never really trusted after that. As I got older the scenario hunted me. Thinking my God, a man whom I thought of as a grandfather, stole my innocence and betrayed my trust. Speaking of trust, the two people that you should be able to trust are your parents. The two most impressionable human beings in your life, your mother and father, are suppose to guide you and protect you at all times. They should also be keen on your likes and dislikes, and not force things on you or want you to live their life. I guess my mother wanted to be a ballerina at one point in time, so she figured that I would to. There I was dressed in a ballerinas outfit, performing the swan dance in front of an auditorium. Earth swallow me now. If I could have jumped inside a volcano and had the larva disintegrate my every being, I would have prefer that, than being there on that stage. Mother dear, if you only new that karate or judo, was more my style, rather than modern dance and ballet. You could have saved yourself lots of money, and both of us from the embarrassment.

However, God forbid, you would have listened to my request, instead you had this notion that if you involved me in female activities, some of the femininity would rub off. Mother you wasted your time and money, and put me through a world of hurt. To her defense though, she did pay for guitar lessons, which I will forever be grateful. I loved to sing and play the guitar. It was my therapy, my escape from this wicked world we live in. I soon discovered I had a talent. I could sing, write and now play the guitar. This new found hobby created a balance in my life. Now, I had a vehicle to express my emotions. I could write what I felt, put a melody to it, and tell the world the pain I was in. Of coarse no one really listened, but it made me feel better. I must say, I was definitely a better guitar player than a ballerina.

There were many painful moments in my life. Many I have repressed, some are vivid as day. There is one that stands out like a sore thumb. The time I got my period. I was in junior high, in the middle of a science class. I felt this trickling sensation between my legs. Then an odor, that I had never experienced before. Class was almost over, so instead of rushing to the bathroom and interrupting class, I figured it could wait till I got home. I took my clothes off, and jumped in the shower. My pants and panties were full of blood, and there was more blood trickling down my legs. I screamed, "mother come to the bathroom, I think I am hurt." She laughed, and said you are finally a women. You are having your period. I never really thought of myself as a women, I tried so hard to ignore the facts. My breast, my genitals, and now this curse, this dreaded time of month, they have been talking about, has finally arrived. What am I suppose to do, jump for joy, rejoice. That now, I have finally reached a mile stone in my life, which places the stamp of approval, of my gender. No thanks, I don't want this, take it back. Mother had this grin on her face, this look of contentment, as if now I belonged to her club, the mother daughter womanly club. One more thing to talk about, one more thing to have in common. Here have these pads, they will keep you dry. To think I had to bare this monthly thing for 25 years, the cramps, the pads, the whole premenstrual saga that connects me to a woman's world. The more I think about it, how I hated it so. No one should have to go through that. To think that being transgender is thought of as a sin, has anyone bothered to think, that being in the wrong body is a crime. Death is appealing to those of us, who are encased in the wrong shell, who are trapped in a flesh of darkness, that reputes and sickens us to the point of madness. Heavenly father spare us the anguish, and let us come home if we cant feel at peace in our own skin.

Adolescence
The Teenage Years

As Cher quotes in her song: "If I can turn back time", this would definitely be the time I would turn back too. 1980, it was my junior year in Coronado High school. I would give my right arm, to go back there as Mark. Maritza really made a mess of it. Awkward, messy, introverted, and unhappy, all words that reflected my feelings during those years. I didn't like guys, so I didn't date them, couldn't really date girls, unless you wanted to come out as a lesbian, and be outcast by your peers. They were hard and painful years of frustration and self loathing. I guess that is why I took up acting, to pretend to be someone else. Actors get to play roles. I wanted to be someone else.

There in my drama world, I could be whom I wanted. I pretended to be Leif Garett, a popular teenage idol at that time. Denise my first love, was Farrah Faccet, one of Charles angels. Leif met Farah and of coarse fell in love. As I mentioned earlier in the book. Denise and I became best of friends, after a while intimacy set in, but in order to handle the situation, we reverted to role playing. Something that was easy for both us, being we were actors an all. It was an escape, so that we wouldn't have to face reality, that I was Maritza and she was Denise. Deep inside she loved me, but could not get passed the idea that I was a female. How different life would be now. I am a happily married man, but the thought of having the chance, to be a male in high school, creates an energy in my spine that tingles all the way down to my toes. The chance to have gone through puberty, then, as a man, and with a male genitalia is priceless. But what is that saying? No use crying over spilled milk. There are times I feel, I have blocked parts of my life. Call it a defense mechanism. Sitting here writing this book, tends to create a strain, while searching for memories of my past. Looking back, one memory is vivid, the time I had an encounter with our maid. I entered her room one summer night, in El Paso Texas, looking to fulfill a sexual fantasy. Lupita was an eighteen year old Mexican girl, who worked and live in our home. She had crossed the border to help her family, by sending them money that she earned as a live in maid. I had my eyes on her for quite a while now, but again, my handicap of being a female, impede me at first, from approaching her. I was like a teenage boy with raving hormones, with a crush on his house keeper. After a while, I developed the courage and entered her room while she slept. I proceeded to touch her, slow and gentle at first, I was hoping she would not awaken. I became excited, her breathing became heavier and her heart raced. I thought to myself, she is becoming aroused, as I caressed her breast, while outlining her nipples with my tongue. Yet, no signs of waking up, this went on, it seemed like an eternity. My hands wondered below her waist, I rubbed her clitoris, feeling it throbbing between my fingers. I tired out, and left the room. The next day, I was curious if she had felt what I had done. "My God you would have to been dead, not to have felt anything." I noticed she tried to avoid me. Making no eye contact, or for that matter, giving me the time of day. Finally, I couldn't bare it any longer. I asked her, "Lupita," did you feel what I did to you last night? Her head tilted down towards the floor, she muttered, yes. She appeared to have been ashamed, as if it was wrong to have enjoyed the pleasure I gave her. I approached her, held her hand, and assured her it was alright. No one needed to know, it was our secret. From that moment on, Lupita an I were lovers. I was thirteen years old, she was my first girl friend, my first lover. We hid it from everyone. There were many nights of passion, all under my parents roof. Lupita had a boyfriend back home, after a while she stopped writing him. She fell in love with me, I was her boyfriend now. Sadly, I out grew Lupita. I wanted to experiment with other girls. She was very jealous and very possessive. After awhile, she could not bare the pain, and left our household. She was broken hearted, I never meant to hurt her, but how many times have we hurt someone with out intending to. I was young, not ready for a full commitment.

In my adolescent years, I had many awkward moments. I was a loner, and had a hard time dealing with my peers. I could not relate to anyone. I new I was not gay, not that there is anything wrong with that. What I felt was different, I felt I was a teenage boy, ready and willing to have a girl friend. How do you tell your peers that you are a boy trapped in a females body. You don't, you suffer in silence, and bare the pain. This made my high school years, unbearable. I went through the motions. I did have a handful of friends. They were eccentric, and different like me. They were into the arts and music which was the only common denominator I had with others that allowed me, to make connections in this world. I had a band, I was the lead singer and rhythm guitar player. We had gigs, birthday parties, weddings, and such, it was fun. It was one of the very few good memories I had. My music was my escape, it allowed me to have some form of sanity. Some common grounds with humanity, a way to communicate, to reach out, and give people a little bit of me. Sing boy sing, pour your little heart out. Let the rhythm run through your veins. Pluck the strings to your steel guitar, let the love flow through your soul, as you play for others to enjoy, as you give them all you know. Let the world feel your pain, as your write the songs that show, the hurt, and sorrow of your world.

A Transgender' Turmoil

Inside a person, there are many emotions and feelings that are kept deep, trapped and hidden from the surface. We all have our inner demons. We all had dysfunctional families, and had to face our fears one way or the other. In a transgender world however, we get mocked by our homosexual brothers and sisters, because we are looked upon as outcast, rebellious, and devious individuals, who do not conform. In the straight world we are also made fun of, ridiculed and not accepted. We really live in a no mans land. So when coming out, or expressing our true nature, we deal with many obstacles and embarrassments. I am a man who was born in a female body. When growing up, looking in the mirror was painful. It deceived me, it lied. I was not the image that appeared before me. Maritza, would comb her hair, brush her teeth, wash her face, all in front of this God forsaken mirror. An object of deception, it created self hatred towards my being. If I didn't look in the mirror, I was someone else. But what do you, go break every mirror in your path? You are looked upon as a con artist, when you are trying to pass. A common term used amongst transgender individuals, who have not had their surgeries, or have begun there hormonal treatments. We bind our breast, wear baggy clothes, all to be able to blend in with society. There were many embarrassing moments, from using the toilet, to engaging in a conversation with the opposite sex. Will we be revealed, will they know that we were once born females? We live in constant fear. This should not be. Open up your hearts fellow being, make our journeys easier. Let us take our baby steps into this world as we carefully create our inner soul, with our outer appearance. Help guide us along, teach us what we need to learn. Like a parent teaches their child the ways of life. I never new how to be a man. I new I felt like one, but I was not armed with the skills, since I was taught to be a woman. Do not judge us, for we are but a mere product of a hormonal mix up, a brain and body miscommunication. Be gentle, and understanding, for we have our own battles to face. Please don't add unnecessary friction to our journeys. Be kind and loving, for this my friends could be an issue in your life. You all have families, brothers, sisters, sons, daughters, and grandkids. Its like playing Russian roulette, any ones brain could be affected.

A transgender world is a lonely world. We cry in silence, hiding our scars, our imperfections. We die everyday, as we get buried by our families, who swear never to speak to us again. We lose our jobs, the roofs over our heads, constantly being discriminated against. Suicide becomes our only outlet, when living in this cruel world is no longer an option. If we survive our own suicide attempts, then others that loath us, manage to complete the job. What a way to live. What a life we lead. You say we bring this upon ourselves. Walk a mile in our shoes, see what our options are. Live in our hell, trapped in someone else's body. This is not a sin, a crime, nor is it deviant behavior. This is a birth defect, created in our mothers' womb, at 8 weeks gestation. Our brains and our bodies failed to communicate. We are human beings with feelings, all we ask is for respect, to mend our birth defects. God created all living creators, I plead with you, to please stop hating and start understanding. Open up your hearts and minds, and just realize, we are Gods children too.

My Transition

I have tried to lead a so called "normal life," in my female body. From getting married to a man, to attempting artificial insemination to bare a child. All things to fight this curse that I have been given. I tried to embrace my female breast, curves, and genitalia. All attempts ended in failure. I prayed to my heavenly father, to please take the thought out of my mind. That if he felt, what I wanted to pursue, a sex change, was wrong, to make it difficult for me. My lord guided me, and made my transition easy. He answered my prayers. I have nothing to be ashamed of, the one I have to face is my maker, and if my maker is ok with my decision, then that's all that matters.

The church needs to accept and embrace us. We are God's creation. We are here to show you, how lucky you are, that you are whole and complete, both on the inside and out. Do not judge, for judging is a sin. Accept us, and free yourself from your own inner turmoil. Embrace us, as we are unique. You should feel lucky, that you got to know, and learn from one of us. That your path met ours. That you got to experience our love, our passion, for no one will ever love you, like we do. We understand your gender, since we had the blessing to live our life as both. We are in tune with both our energies, our yin and yang, and have managed to create a balance as part of our camouflage. We are from Venus and mars, and now have united both planets to live in harmony. My transition has been one hell of a journey. I have learned to live, communicate, and express my emotions, as I have never before. I have grown as an individual, managed to love myself, one thing I new nothing about, before. I have buried Maritza, but she will always have a special place in my heart. She almost destroyed and managed to kill us. Mark is strong, a survivor. He has taken Maritza's positive traits and learned from her mistakes. Her self destructive path, has edged a trail of emotions which now surfaced to help others deal with theirs. I pledge myself, as a transsexual man, to help my little brothers and sisters, bringing peace in to their lives. I will become an advocate, an educator, I will not stop, until I feel we have made our mark here on earth.

Hormones, therapy, surgery, all words that explain a transsexuals journey. We will survive, we will prevail. The outside will match the inside. Its our task, its our mission. The art work is in progress. Like a canvas, fresh and ready to be painted, we lay before our doctors, to help us mend our birth defects. We trust that these men and women, whom we count on, will take on the challenge and make us right.

Science needs to advance. The creation of a male penis is still not perfected. I want nothing more, than to wake up with a hard on, and to ejaculate inside my wife. To stand up and urinate like a man. These are things that lay heavy on my mind. Although, I look and feel like a man, I am still missing an important component to the equation, a dick, something many man take for granted, or do they? I want what is rightfully mine. To complete my transition, I need a phallus. Our sisters who transitioned are able to enjoy having a vagina. Why is it so difficult to create a penis. I challenge the medical community to take interest and facilitate the construction of fully functional penis. I know its not the cure for cancer, but for us transsexual men, it might as well be.

My Losses and Gains

I once had a voice like an angel, I sang like a sparrow, my talents were heavenly. Testosterone changed my voice. I went through puberty at 39 years of age. Like a teenage boy, my voice cracked with every syllable I spoke. If there were to be a grievance in my transition, losing the ability to sing would be one of them. Maritzas' voice, got her much needed attention and recognition. She sang her little heart out, entertaining the world with her music. When Mark took over Maritzas' body, her voice went with her. I could no longer sing. This brought sadness to my heart. But its something I will have to live with, to be able to be the man, I was born to be. My voice is now deep. I can't hold a tune if my life depended on it. This is something that is very difficult for me to deal with. Since my identity growing up, relied soley on my singing. I guess it's the price I have to pay, to allow Mark the man to take his thrown. Maybe God gave Maritza a voice, to help us bare the pain, of being in the wrong body. Another so call loss, is my hair. I once had very thick and curly long hair. I now have thin and a balding head. All a buy product of testosterone, which converts to

DHT, a hair follicle deactivator, that chockes the hair shaft, making it thin, and eventually falling off. Genetics plays a major role on who will keep their hair or who will lose it .

There are far more gains than loses in my quest to aline my brain with my body. For starters, I am my true self. For the first time in my life, I know what happiness is. The clothes I wear feel right, the hair all over my body belongs. I love the feel of my face when I shave. The muscles and strength I have acquired, feels amazing. I look in the mirror now and become mesmerized by the reflection I see. The respect that I get from people, as I demonstrate my authority is beyond words. I am a man, no longer looked at as weak, or timid. I walk like a roman soldier with my shoulders squared and my head high. I feel empowered, ready to face the world. Nothing to fear, I am king of my castle. This is a man's world no doubt, no disrespect to our ladies, I love them, and think they are stronger than we give them credit for. They help us embrace our strength. We are but mere children, looking to impress and conquer the love of our maiden. I love the feel of my wife, her touch, her stare, the smell of her skin and hair. The way women make us men feel is priceless. We are the lion, the daddy, the papi, they can really boost our ego. There is nothing like being a man, walking with our heads held high and ready for battle. Yes there are many gains of my transition. I have entered a new world a new ball game.

What a feeling of mastery, control, there is nothing like it. What a blessing to have had the opportunity, in one life time, to live a dream. To be the man that I have always dreamt of being. I Mark Angelo Cummings, can stand before you all, and say that I am the happiest man alive. I have created my destiny, shaped my world, build my own castle and now, I am riding my own horse. I have the perfect wife, and the most amazing life, and I am able to share it with you, my readers, my confidants. This is my therapy, telling my story to the world. Sharing my thoughts, my feelings, bringing my message to the table. Everything in life has its pros and cons. You face it, and balance the check book. I have to say the pros out ways the cons. This was the right decision for me, no questions about it. No regrets, no looking back, its onward and forwards to the end.

Sexuality and Gender

Why must people categorize everything into a little box, as if it were one big umbrella. If you are transsexual, then you must be a homosexual? Wrong, let me explain. Sexuality and gender are two different things. Who you want to go to bed with, and what you feel you are, as an individual, are opposing poles like the north and the south. My sister is a proud lesbian. She likes her body, with the exception of a few extra pounds that she is carrying around, nevertheless, she does not want to be a man. However, she loves women. The thought of being intimate with a man, repulses her. She looks in the mirror and it feel right. No dysphoria there. My sister felt betrayed when she learned of my decision of changing my sex. We were very close, since we both shared the love for women. So obviously, when she learned that I would soon become the enemy, it caused a little friction in our relationship. Since then we have worked out our differences, and she respects and understands my decision. There are many homosexuals who are fine with their bodies. They enjoy having sex with the same sex, but do not feel misaligned with their body and mind. Transsexuals on the other hand, come in all shapes and sizes. For instance, there are transgender who are bisexual, homosexuals, or just plain heterosexual. I know its confusing, but follow me here. A man who was born with gender dysphoria, goes through his entire life, wanting to be a female. Gets married, has children, but after a while, he cannot bare the pain. He tells his wife, he is going to become a women, and has his surgeries. He decides to stays with his wife, even after his transition. He still loves her, and enjoys having sex with her. This transsexual women is a lesbian, who feels that she is a women, corrected her birth defect, and now lives happily every after. Following me? The Other case scenario, goes like this. A man born with gender dysphoria, marries, has kids, decides he is in the wrong body, tell his wife, leaves her to be with a man. He is now a heterosexual/transsexual woman. I know its confusing, but the bottom line is, its about the gender, not about the sex. Its who you feel you are inside.

Let me point out, I have nothing against gays, lesbians or bisexuals. I wish the world would get over their hang up, of who goes to bed with who. Sex is not a crime, unless you are a child molester, then you need psychological intervention. We need to learn to look at peoples hearts, and not their genitals. As I once heard a preacher man quote, a square peg cannot fit in a round one, what in the world does it matter. Love is love, whatever shape, color or gender it comes in. The universe will not fall apart if two men fall in love, get married and have sex. There are definitely bigger and worst things to worry about. Like innocent people dying in war, modern day slavery taking place today, to make corporations bigger and richer. Pharmaceutical companies poisoning us to make a buck, religious leaders making hateful comments to make themselves feel better. Think about it, if you really paid close attention to what you are saying, that if two women or two men sleep with each other, the world will come to an end. What is so wrong with that. Its two human beings giving each other love and pleasure. Two consenting adults, that's all, nothing wrong with that. Also, who died and made you the judge. God is the only one we need to face, on judgment day, not pastor Bob, nor sister Ellen. Stop being nosy, and prying into peoples business. What anyone does in their bedroom, should stay in their bedroom. Uncle Sam, the President, congress, the supreme courts, have no right to pry, make laws, point fingers and say that, anyone's sexual preference is wrong. So grow up and get a life. We are way past the eighteenth century. We need to move on, open our minds and hearts, and realize that being different is ok. Lets teach unconditional love, lets remove the guilt, open the church to everyone, and make it a place of understanding. That is what our heavenly father wants for his children, for us to get along. No more fighting, no more name calling. Lets learn to respect, and accept our differences. Feel how freeing it really is when you allow your heart to forgive, when you stop creating walls between each other. We are all the same, brothers and sisters struggling to survive on a daily basis, in this world filled with hate, diseases, hunger, poverty and lies. Lets break down the barriers, lets have each others back, and do what we are suppose to do, love each other without conditions. That my friends is what its all about.

The Many Faces of Mark

I am who I am, always have been, and always will be. The costumes have changed through the years, but the goal, and the focus has always been the same. Some of the relationships I have had, have helped shape the person I am today. I truly believe that everyone that comes into our lives are there for a reason. Few are there to teach, while others are there to learn. Its a class room our world, things don't just happen. There is a method to the madness, a formula to follow. It's all written in the books, from the day you are born to the day you die. Mark has been a victim, I have held that title for many years. Although I have placed it behind me, nevertheless, I was victimized. I was a buy product of our forgotten world. Born cross eyed, sickly, afraid, and with very little strength to hold my own. I was manipulated, and controlled, never speaking out for myself. I would always agree and went along with things, in order not to make waives. This was a learned behavior, stemmed from trying to please my mother. Many of my relationships did not last long, I guess I bored them, I was too pleasing, not enough character for some. Then there was Mark the lover, I was indeed better at that role, I fulfilled a need. I had passion, a fire within that would quench anyone's' thirst for lust and desire. I knew what they liked or disliked, I sensed their every wants and needs. My hands would go were they where needed, my lips explored their every crevice. I was the master of pleasure. Being born two spirited, gave me quite an advantage. I knew what each gender desired, I knew how to please my mate. As the years went buy, I learned to build character, to not rely on giving pleasure, in order to be desired or needed. My spiritual side developed, I became in tune with my surroundings. I now cultivate my third sense in other ways, to heal, to bring joyous thought into peoples minds. I don't regret any of the things I have done, for they have made me who I am today. Looking back the journey has been inspiring, and bold. Every lover I have ever had, has left a mark in my soul, has help bring together the pieces to the puzzle. No question in my mind that I carry a token of each of them in my soul, a collective collage of memories and feelings, all in one.

I was fresh out of high school, and had return home to Miami. My parents finally separated and were on the verge of divorce. Can't say I didn't see it coming. Dad and his drinking, mom and her nagging, two combinations that could start a nuclear war. I was staying with my grandmother at the time, God bless her she meant well, but if I had to stay one more day cooped up in her apartment, I would have definitely jumped from her balcony. I had to find a job, I needed to get out of her place. But since I didn't have a car, or much experience in the work force, it led to constant rejection during my job interviews. I had to do something desperate, and after watching Goldie Hawn in Private Benjermin, the Army sounded like the thing to do. Yep, I enlisted, I was merely seventeen years old when Uncle Sam got a hold of me. Well it wasn't exactly paradise, nor did I have the good old time Goldie Hawn appeared to have, while she perused her self throughout the barracks. It was an experience though, from getting caught making out with another girl, which nearly got me in the stockade, to spending half my days kissing the ground while attempting the famous pushups. I have never seen an operation so into making people kiss the floor. The sergeant had it out for me from the very start. So needles to say, I mastered the pushups. I guess the best part of being in the Army was the fact that I was surrounded by females. Well, I can't say it was a waste of time, I learned to polish my shoes, make a killer bed, and to walk really fast. Oh, I got to shoot an M-16, and became pretty efficient in fighting. Things that prepare you for the real world.

Thinking back, I went through the Disco face, where every chance I had, I hit the bars. The gay bars to be exact. Of coarse, the drugs and alcohol were a staple in my life, it was the thing to do, it helped mask the pain. Girl after girl, nothing satisfied me. It was my way of life then, empty, void and meaningless. Along the way, I manage to have some long term relationships, trying to find my place in this world. But the mirror wasn't making any sense, not any time soon. I hooked up with many different types of girls, some had children, some not. I wanted to find the family life, and feel complete as a man, "in a female body." Finding one self, is rather difficult as a young adult. Add the fact that you feel your body isn't yours, makes it even harder. It was like wearing a really bad Halloween costume, or being imprisoned in someone else's skin. Except you can't take the costume off, nor make bail.

Crack cocaine, just hearing the word, makes my hairs rise. I was so addicted to that drug, that my next door neighbor who actually distributed the stuff, owned all my possessions. After I ran out of money, I started giving her my furniture, jewelry, or anything she would like. After a while, her place looked like mine. I had a love affair with the pipe, that first hit, would light up all the nerves in my brain. You could never get the same feeling afterwards. Yet like an addict, you continue to suck in the air, gasping for every breath and taste of that lethal poison. Down on all fours, looking for pieces that might have fallen on the floor. My hands would shake, my eyes did a dance. I would look out the window, paranoid as hell. It was no life, but it was my life then. I sit hear writing the details, and it's as if, I am writing about someone else. But it was me, the female body was killing me.

I managed to kick the habit, after much prayer and learning that drugs was not going to change me. I decided to moved on, and life took a better turn. I went to college and got a career, at the age of 26. I wanted to help people, so I became an Occupational Therapist. It was a hard six years. At first, I worked and went to school at the same time. Once I got accepted to the program, I had to stop working and dedicate myself as a full time student. I lived with a very nice girl at the time. She was very supportive, and understanding. I cared for her very much, but unfortunately, her love for me was greater than mine. I felt bad, after six years and finishing school, I left her. We had two different paths, like ships passing through the night, we then set sail apart. Because of her, I learned to love myself, some what. She was kind, and her kindness opened up my heart. She was a real good friend, someone I enjoyed spending time with, but in love, I was not.

Then came the doctor, a pleasant girl who I met while working for a reputable pain center. She had her Ph.D. in business administration, and was also in the therapy field. We thought we had a lot in common. Hit it off for a few years. We ran a business together, got involved in bodybuilding and attempted to start a family. I was the brave soul who was going to carry the infant to term, considering her pain tolerance was zero to none, the choice was obvious. So off to the sperm bank we went in search of a donor. We tried several times to get pregnant, in search of that perfect family circle, the perfect life. Luckily I was unable to get pregnant, my insides were not made to carry a child. I guess it was a blessing, since the relationship turned bad. The pain was getting deeper, hiding who I was, was getting harder. I could not continue to hurt people and myself this way. I have been through so many trials and tribulations. I have searched high and low for happiness. The answer was to align my brain with my body. There was no other solution.

The Secret Of The Sexes
Male vs. Female

I can truly say that I have lived a dream. I feel I hold the key to answers relating to gender. I have had the opportunity to experience life as a male and a female. The two are quite different, yet have certain similarities. The game is on. Who will break the silence. Gentle they appear, claiming to be the weaker sex, so they say. Its all an act, a ploy to get their way. They sit back and explore how they could win their battle. Pretending to be sweet and innocent. Keep your eyes open men for they will devour you like the black widow. I know, I have been their and back. They will make you think you are in control. They will bat an eye, and give you a gentle smile, while inside they are planning a plot to take no prisoners. Blaming it on the hormones, they will eat you out of house and home, during that infamous time of the month, while they go from doctor Jeckle to Mrs. Hide. All in the name of the menstrual cycle. Yes it's true, the bloating, P.M.S., and all the tears, but they do have some control. More than they'll let people know. Face it is easier to blame it on that, than to take responsibility for your actions. Pretending to have an orgasm, that is yet a favorite of mine. A quick way out, not wanting to hurt your feelings, instead making you feel like you are the king of the jungle. When really they think, you are merely a cub. It takes a lot to please a woman, you have to think like one, or actually have been one to really get under their skin. Now men, in order to conquer your lady friend, you must balance your male and female side. Don't get me wrong you don't have to polish your nails, or wax your eye brows. Just carefully study their ways, and before you know it, you've cracked the code. You will be well on your way.

The chase, the courtship, all part of the grand scheme. They like the idea of playing the game. If you are too easy, forget it, they lose interest. If you are too hard, no, not down their silly. If you play hard to get, they will jump to the next opponent and forget about you in an instant. Its like fishing you see, you give a little line, then you pull in for the catch. To many flowers, to many gifts, then you are doomed, for all they will want is your gold. A token of affection is all right, but don't over do it bud, its like sugar, too much makes your mouth turn. When it comes to decision making, a democracy is appreciate it, but don't be wishie washy either. They like you stern with some authority, even thought they pretend they don't. The cave man had the idea, to a certain extent. Now I know I am sounding like a male chauvinist pig here, but these things I know, I have been to other side. The key is to make them fall in love. Because even the roughest of the bunch, will submit to your every demand. The question is how do you make them fall in love. Be mysterious, have that suave attitude, but don't over do it. Do win their respect. If they admire you, and think you are all that, then you have it made. Learn to talk their language. Females love to talk, I have a wife, I know. Beside, when estrogen was still flowing through my veins, I was considered Poly the Parrot. I could talk up a storm. Funny enough though, I don't speak much now, I am actually a man of few words. What a difference a change of hormones make.

Go shopping with them, they love that stuff. I know it's torture. I really hate it to the max., but if you are trying to bond with your girl friend, the mall is the place to go. Be one of the girls to her, and she will worship the grounds you walk on. Don't worry you wont have to do it long. Beside, this way you can keep taps on what she spends. Its learning to be her everything, her friend, her lover, her father, and mother. Make her think she can't be without you. Trust me guys, you will have her eating from the palm of your hand.

In bed you must tell her how beautiful she is. The female organ is connected to her feelings and brain. If your girl is upset, you can forget sex. Her G spot is attached to her heart, so romance her, cuddle, caress, kiss, and be all emotional, and you will make her cum like never before. Communication is the key. Oh, one thing more, learn to find her G spot. The flood gates will open, here is the road map. In the vagina opening, place two finger and head north. You will feel a spongy thing, continue to press upward, be gentle, you are not digging for gold. Make a come here motion with your fingers while pressing on the spot. You might have to play around a bit until you find it. This my friends is where it all takes place. Here is another hint, girls like their clitoris rubbed and licked. This, at the same time while stimulating her G spot, will give her multiple pleasurable orgasms beyond her wildest dreams. I know, I give my wife at least 10 at a time.

Now ladies its your turn to learn what make your man tick. Make him think he is the king of the jungle, we love that stuff. Every man has an emperor or king in his brain. We like to feel in control, we like to be worshiped. Make us feel like we are your protector, that you need us to survive. Don't be too clingy though, we don't like to be smothered, either. Let us have our space from time to time, but not too much, or we will find something to occupy our time with. Don't trust your girl friends around us, guys don't hate me, but its true, we think with our other head, when it comes to things like that. Every man has an inner child, who loves to get pampered and spoiled. We are big babies, although we will never admit it. We don't like to talk, so learn to read our minds. Really its not hard, we have several programs, learned them. Don't get hurt or offended, we can only be romantic at first, we like our side of the bed, and don't like to cuddle for long. We can be affectionate at times, but it is not part of our make up, so just remember the courtship, and reminisce on that. We really do love you, we swear, but just because we aren't all over you doesn't mean we don't care. Our hormones only allow is to be all loving when we want to make love. Again, its not our fault, blame it on our hormones.

When we reach an orgasm, lights are out, its a feeling we can't control. I know, as a female, I could have an orgasm, then talk the entire night. As a man, when I come, its lights out, and good night. Can't explain it, its how it is. Some sort of chemical release, that beats any sleeping pill. Here is another advise, play the role game, keep it new, we like new. Have fantasies, it keeps the relationship fresh. Also ladies, don't wear all the junk on your face to bed, like those night creams and stuff. Men like their woman to be pretty all the time, even if the lights are out. Lipstick, its nice when you are going out and stuff, but when we are wanting to be romantic, we don't like the stuff, it rubs off on our face. At least I don't. Maybe its just me, because I hated to wear make up when I was a female, and now when my wife kisses me and she has lip stick on, I can't stand it on me. Ladies please don't talk our ears off, we don't like it when you nag, keep the pitch at a comfort zone, is that too much to ask? To please your man in the sack, takes imagination, and a well thought plan. Men like to watch porn, so they can fantasize. Watch it with them, and pretend you are enjoying too. Live the fantasy through the tube. Play roles in bed, let your imagination run wild. Its about fun, its about going beyond your wildest dreams. Don't be a nun. Keep the lights on, the covers off and let your kinky side go wild. You will keep him coming for more.

All kidding aside, hormones play a major role in our behavior. My thought process has definitely changed since I now have testosterone in my veins. I don't cry at the drop of a hat. My taste in women has definitely changed, and the way I think is no longer the same. It's not that I am not caring, but I have become much harder inside. I once admired a strong physiques, I enjoyed watching female bodybuilders on stage. Now I wouldn't look at them twice. I like women toned but soft and curvy. They need to be feminine and coy.

I think now more than before, and speak allot less. I can make my mind up easier than before. Estrogen can really fluctuate your moods. It torments your every existence, at least it did mine. The war inside my head, prior to my transition, was very debilitating. Over all, Men and women are definitely from two different planets. Testosterone and Estrogen, make the body react in totally different ways. You wonder if God created us that way for a reason. What one has in excess the other is lacking, together they make a great team. To get really philosophical here, you can see that everything in the world has two sides, black and white, night and day, yin and yang, positive and negative, male and female. That is just the way the world is. It cannot be changed. We can however learn to live together, respect our boundaries, and make our stay here on earth as pleasant as possible.

All in all, we can learn to live together in harmony. Just learn to speak each others language, and respect each others wants and needs. Its about compromising that's all. Life can be beautiful if we just learn to get along.

When I Told The Truth

After my transition, I began to live a peaceful and productive life. I blended in nicely, no one would ever imagine I was born a girl. Life was normal, my wife and I ran our business, and went along our daily routine, like you average middle class American. I decided it was time to give back to the world, to come out and share my story. So I agreed to be on The Maury Povich talk show, on national TV, and disclose my gender dsyphoria to the world. I had worked so hard to blend in, to be your average Joe. But now the world will know. I figured what was so special about blending in. I have to help others like myself find their place in this world. I have to open peoples minds and hearts by telling my story. The experience was unbelievable. New York City, was amazing. I had not been on an airplane since 1991, since I had a fear of flying. But not even my fear would stop me now. I had to disclose my secret to those who did not know. There were many people who only new me as Mark. Now they will know the truth. One of the greatest things about this trip was meeting others like me, who will also tell their story. The energy was invigorating, the whole experience changed my life. I have a purpose now. I will tell everyone that comes my way, I will create awareness. I must say the reactions I got varied. Some people thought I was joking, when I told them. When they realized I was telling them the truth, they didn't know what to do with the information. The expressions on their face was priceless. They all seem to go through the same stages. First disbelief, then shock, followed by curiosity, and finally acceptance. I feel I have helped many people open up their minds. They are now a little more tolerant of others. They all tend to see me as a very caring and loving person, since I have always given all of me, in my work, and in my personal life. Those that know me, love and respect me, found it hard to judge me, I felt they had no choice but to understand. They admired my courage, my life altering decision. Knowing my character, they new I had done the right thing. I want the world to look at my transsexual brothers and sisters, with the same respect, love and admiration. We are an inspiration to man kind.

I thank you heavenly father for allowing me to share my story, the chapters of my life. I thank you my readers, friends, family and all that know me, especially my wife for being part and helping my journey along. I hope I have made your reading experience unique, that I have brought a smile to your face, and a joyful tear in your eyes. I Mark Angelo Cummings hope to make a mark in this universe, and forever be part of your lives. Please think of me when you feel prejudice entering your hearts. When you think you are about to hate, or create a negative thought, remember what you've read, and open up your soul. I love you world, and I thank you for the opportunity to live. To allow each day that passes by, to be a good day, to grow and help others grow with me. I encourage my transsexaul family to speak out, don't hide or just blend in, we are beautiful people with much to say. We need to educate others, let them know who we are and that we exist. That is the only way we will make strides and change this prejudice world we live in.

To the medical community I say, educate yourselves about our condition. Find ways to help us become more complete physically, so that we can feel whole emotionally. It can't be that hard to recreate a penis, one that functions like every man alive dreams of having. To our government I challenge you to be compassionate, get involved in our fight and quest. Let your people live in a world that has no boundaries, obstacles nor limits. Help us be, who we were meant to be, by funding research, motivating science to educate the masses, on a condition that can no longer be hidden. Israel made a law in 1987, that acknowledges Gender Dysphoria as an error of nature. They pay and help transexuals with their surgeries and transition. Do they have a more compasionate government than ours? Gender Dysphoria is real, gender identity disorder is no joke. There are millions of us out there, in need of body and mind alignment. To the church I say pray to your creator to give you wisdom, tolerance and acceptance in your hearts. Stop the bigotry, the hatred, the judging, lets leave the judging for the man upstairs. To my parents I say thank you. I hope I have made you both proud. I hold no grudges, nor hate in my heart, for you two brought into this world a man, who through his love and compassion, hopes to change the world one day. Mother I love you, and although you feel you have lost a daughter, she was never really there. You however, failed to see your son Mark, he has always been there by your side. Loving and longing for your love. To my siblings, thank you for your love and understanding, you are my heart and soul, my two little angels, that will always be a part of me. Finally, to my wife I say, baby it doesn't get better than this. I hope I can always fulfill you in every way. That I can return the love and understanding you provide me. I pray that our Lord will give us much health, and a long life to share together, till death do us part. This book has been such a therapeutic journey for me. I have cried, laughed and reflected on every page and chapter I wrote. I now leave you with this thought: "This world is ever changing, it rotates on its axis since the beginning of time. Our creator had dreams and hopes for us all. One of which was, for his children to love, laugh and play together, as good brothers and sisters should. He is our father, the one that we will have to face on judgment day. We are the children who need to learn to play and love in peace. Lets make our father proud…"

Mark's Poems

My thoughts

In this world we live in, in these times that have come along, we have lost the true meaning of love. Unconditioned, without strings, without questions or without the need to defend it. So judgmental are we, so much we ask in return. Yet we have churches, we have Temples, because we believe this is our salvation. Go pray, go pay, and we will have a place in heaven, so they say. How hypocritical are we, we lay laws of the land, to have others follow our commands. Yet behind close doors there are so many things that we do wrong. Hush - hush, do as I say, not as I do, oh I get it, the laws don't pertain to you. Priests, Pastors, Rabbis, law makers, law enforcers, government and all, what is wrong with our world today, can we all learn to get along. Like children we are, can't play together, can't seem to sing the same songs. Killing each other, our young and the weak, all for some crude oil and stupid technicalities. Mother Nature is attacking the earth, she is so ashamed of us all, we have destroyed our ozone, environment and our precious world. And what about the death penalty, I ask? Oh, I see, we believe, Its the right thing to keep the peace. But why I ask? And they reply, we don't want to pay for them to be behind bars. So it's easier and less to pay, if we killed the defected, the once that have gone stray. How loving, how humanitarian is this. Christianity, yeah I get, its about the money and greed. Raise your arms in the air and do some fancy chant, have bible studies every week, and you'll have plenty of money in the bank. So they say its Gods wrath, its Gods way, homosexuals and transsexuals most pay. Come on people get a grip, what is sin? Who created the word and it's meaning? Oh, right the Bible, the scripts from the past, some homophobic prophet who didn't like it up the ass. What's the harm, who are they hurting, they have more fashion sense than you and your aunt Rosy. Oh I get it, they think children will be molested by Homo's and queers, no I don't think so, there not pedophiles, nor do they enjoy living in fear. Look at your priests, pastors and the lot, be more afraid of them then of us. If you don't get it by now, that being different is not wrong, it's what's inside your heart and soul, that's what counts, that is all. Yes God, the Universe, the almighty power wants us to love, not hate, live and let live, not kill, nor judge and learn to live with each other in this crazy game we call life. Stop the power struggles, stop the greed; that's what I am talking about, not extremes, to respect and love thy neighbor and do not judge, love unconditionally. Because when judgment day comes along, then maybe, just maybe you might see the gates of heaven and not the pit of hell and fall. Look around you the world is falling, and its due to our nature, hatred, greed, control, barbarians we are, must see blood, flesh and crushed skulls. False prophets, religion now becoming tainted with politics. Take a breath, relax, due no harm, we are all in it together, remember this once and for all. In the name of the father, the son and the holy ghost, get a life redeem yourself and drop the ball. Tolerance, respect, and the ability to flow as one nation, humankind will be instinct if not changed, and learn that differences are beautiful, and not a sin. Love knows no color or gender, there are no rules to its expression. Why must we categorize and limit everything we touch. Why does every puzzle piece have to fit, different is good, different is beautiful. That is what makes the colors of the rainbow unique, no two people should ever be alike, the world is a collage, let it flow, let it be. Gay marriage will not end civilization as we know it, but our backward mentally, the need to hurt each other, war, and the love of money will. The sanction of marriage, you say, what sanction? Britney Spears and half of Hollywood's marriages and the worlds are so holy? They end up in divorce, bringing to this world a bunch of dysfunctional children, abandon, unhappy, and mentally crushed. Yet we want to ban abortion to create more births. Are we not over populated already, are there not enough orphans to feed, or does mother nature half to create further destruction to decline the numbers and create more grief. Think get it right, with all your degrees and all your might, so righteous, so moral you feel, of coarse, only for your convenience and your preferences, go on throw the first stone, I dare you, you can't, can you, I know.

Just

The scars that he bares will forever be there, but its just a reminder of the struggles his been through. No one to blame, no one to change, it's just how it is, its his story his fate. In a perfect world in a perfect place, he would have been the man he was born to be. Yet you try to judge, and you try to change him, but you can't take away the man that he was intended to be, the man in his brain. Now you look in the mirror and justify, are you content with what you see on the inside and out. If the answer is yes, then you can feel really blessed, because for some of us though the mirror makes no sense. Yet you think we are a sin, and you think that we lie, when we try desperately to match the out with the inside. Just look inside your heart and ask yourself this, why are there so many deaths, why all those awful hate crimes. Is that not a sin is that not a crime, is that what god intended for his children to cry. Brothers and sisters, can't you plainly see, we were born to help you, to set you free to help you realize how lucky you are, that you are whole and complete both in and outside. So all that we ask is to please let us be, and for once in a while to learn to count your blessings. Hear our cry, feel our pain, we want whole, and feel not a shame. We yearn despertaley to be, just, the same.

Online Resources

www.LynnConway.com

www.gendertree.com

About The Author

Mark Angelo Cummings is an Occupational Therapist who is the owner of Bodies Under Construction, Inc. He is well respected in his community, and is planning to change how society in general looks at transsexuals and gender dysphoria. He can be reached via email at argomar@bellsouth.net or visit his website at www.bodiesunderconstructiononline.com.